Do You Really Want to Skate on Thin Ice?

A Book about States of Matter

WRITTEN BY DANIEL D. MAURER · ILLUSTRATED BY TERESA ALBERINI

ADVENTURES IN

SCIENCE

ADVENTURES IN

AMICUS ILLUSTRATED
is published by Amicus
P.O. Box 1329, Mankato, MN 56002
www.amicuspublishing.us

Copyright © 2017 Amicus.
International copyright reserved in all countries.
No part of this book may be reproduced in any form
without written permission from the publisher.

Paperback edition printed by RiverStream Publishing in arrangement with Amicus.
ISBN 978-1-62243-351-3 (paperback)

Library of Congress Cataloging-in-Publication Data
Names: Maurer, Daniel D., 1971- author. | Alberini, Teresa, illustrator.
Title: Do you really want to skate on thin ice? : a book about states of
matter / by Daniel D. Maurer ; illustrated by Teresa Alberini.
Description: Mankato, MN : Amicus, [2017] | Series: Adventures in science |
Series: Amicus illustrated | Audience: K to grade 3. |
Includes bibliographical references and index.
Identifiers: LCCN 2015047944 (print) | LCCN 2015049183 (ebook) |
ISBN 9781607539582 (library binding : alk. paper) | ISBN 9781681510705 (eBook)
Subjects: LCSH: Matter—Properties—Juvenile literature. |
Ice—Juvenile literature. | Water—Juvenile literature. |
Science—Study and teaching (Elementary)—Juvenile literature.
Classification: LCC QC926.37 .M385 2017 (print) |
LCC QC926.37 (ebook) | DDC 530.4—dc23
LC record available at http://lccn.loc.gov/2015047944

Editor: Rebecca Glaser
Designer: Kathleen Petelinsek

Printed in the United States of America at
Corporate Graphics in North Mankato, Minnesota.

HC 10 9 8 7 6 5 4 3 2 1
PB 10 9 8 7 6 5 4 3 2 1

ABOUT THE AUTHOR

Daniel D. Maurer writes for both children and adults and lives in Saint Paul, Minnesota with his wife, two boys, two cats, and one dog. They all dig science together. Visit *www.danthestoryman.com* to learn more.

ABOUT THE ILLUSTRATOR

Teresa Alberini has always loved painting and drawing. She attended the Academy of Fine Arts in Florence, Italy, and she now lives and works as an illustrator in a small town on the Italian coast. Visit her on the web at *www.teresaalberini.com.*

Everything around you is made of matter. The pond by your friend's house, the trees, and your ice skates are made of matter. You and your friend are made of matter. Even the air you breathe is matter.

You will find matter in different states. In summer,
the pond is a liquid. But in the cold winter, water
freezes into a solid. Then you can go ice-skating!

Water freezes at 32 degrees Fahrenheit (0°Celsius). It turns into solid ice. But if it warms up a little, the ice will start melting back into a liquid. Do you really want to skate on thin ice?

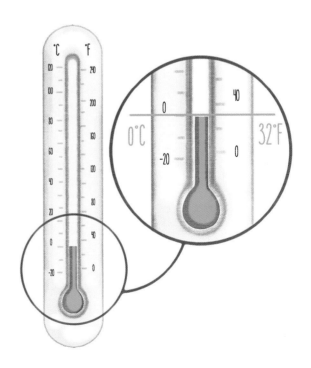

Oh no! When the ice cracks, you fall into the liquid water below. Luckily, the water isn't too deep. Deep, cold water is dangerous!

Why is there water below the ice? The pond only
freezes on the surface—and ice floats on the water.

You'd better go dry off—and quickly, before your clothes freeze in the cold air.

Air is a mixture of gases, which are another state of matter. Gases are invisible.

When your clothes dry, where does the water go? The heat in the house warms up the water enough that the water turns into a gas, or evaporates. Usually you can't see evaporation. But you know it's happening because your clothes will get dry.

Some hot cocoa will help you warm up, too. Boiling is another way to change a liquid to a gas. Water boils at 212° Fahrenheit or 100° Celsius.

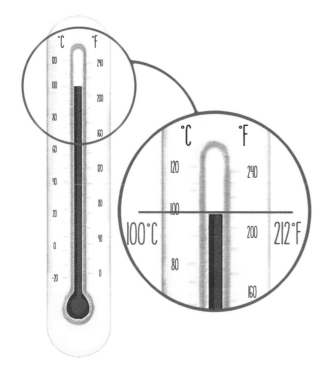

As the steam escapes from the kettle, it is water as a gas, or water vapor. When the water vapor first boils out of the kettle, you can't see it.

When the vapor cools a bit in the air, it condenses into tiny water droplets. These tiny droplets make up the "cloud" you see above your boiling teakettle. You can also see condensation inside your cocoa mug.

What about something to eat? How about popcorn? Popcorn uses a change in the state of matter to make it pop.

There is water inside each kernel of popcorn. As the popcorn is heated, the water turns into steam. The steam expands and the kernel explodes!

How about melting butter for the popcorn? Butter has different states too! Butter can be solid or it can be liquid— if you heat it.

You really don't want to skate on thin ice. But now you know how states of matter change! Some even taste good!

Some solids can change into liquids. They melt when they are heated. Try making these yummy treats to see how chocolate changes states.

WHAT YOU NEED:

- One solid chocolate bar
- Microwave-safe bowl
- Hot pads
- Graham crackers
- Tray with waxed paper

WHAT YOU DO:

1. Break the chocolate bar into pieces and put them in the bowl.
2. With the help of an adult, melt the chocolate in the microwave. Start with one minute. Add more time, if needed. Now that it's melted, it's a liquid.
3. Use the hot pads to remove the bowl. Be careful—it's hot! Dip the graham crackers in the liquid chocolate.
4. Set the graham crackers on the tray and let the chocolate cool before you eat them. As it cools, the chocolate will change back into a solid.
5. What are the differences between liquid chocolate and solid chocolate?

Fruit juice can change states of matter too. Freeze juice to make a tasty solid, frozen pop. Then measure how fast it melts when you eat it.

JUICE POPS FREEZE & THAW-O-RAMA

WHAT YOU NEED:

- Ice cube tray
- Pop sticks
- Aluminum foil
- Fruit juice
- Stopwatch

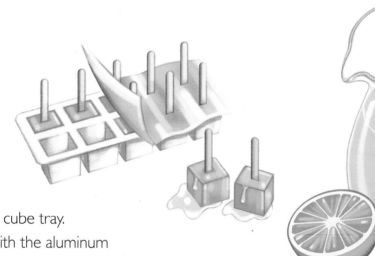

WHAT YOU DO:

1. Pour the juice into the ice cube tray.
2. Carefully cover the tray with the aluminum foil so it fits tightly on top.
3. Poke one pop stick into each "cube" through the foil.
4. Put the ice cube tray in the freezer for at least two hours.
5. Carefully remove the foil, and enjoy a juice pop! The heat in your mouth will melt the pop as you eat it. Use the stopwatch to measure how long it takes to melt.
6. Try putting one pop in a bowl on the counter. Does it melt faster or slower than the one you ate?

GLOSSARY

boil—To heat a liquid so that it bubbles and turns into a gas.

condense—To change from a gas into a liquid, usually because of cooling.

evaporate—To change from a liquid into a gas, usually because of heating.

freeze—To cool something enough that it changes from a liquid to a solid.

gas—A state of matter that expands to fill any space that contains it. Common gases are steam and air.

liquid—A state of matter that flows into the shape of its container. Water is the most common liquid on Earth.

matter—Something that has weight and takes up space.

melt—To change something from a solid to a liquid by heating it.

solid—A state of matter that is stiff and holds its shape. Common solids are ice, steel, wood, plastic, and glass.

water vapor—Water in a gas state; water vapor is invisible. It is also called steam.

READ MORE

Hanson-Harding, Alexandra. **What Is Matter?** New York: Britannica Educational Publishing/Rosen, 2015.

Larson, Karen. **Changing Matter**. Huntington Beach, Calif.: Teacher Created Materials, 2015.

Weakland, Mark. **The Solid Truth about Matter**. Mankato, Minn.: Capstone Press, 2013.

WEBSITES

PBS Kids: Geyser Surpriser
http://pbskids.org/fetch/games/geyser/game.html
This game shows how underground water boils and shoots out of a geyser.

States of Matter | ABCya!
http://www.abcya.com/states_of_matter.htm
Learn about solids, liquids, and gases, and then sort objects into the correct category.

**States of Matter
(Science Trek: Idaho Public Television)**
http://idahoptv.org/sciencetrek/topics/matter/index.cfm
Watch a short video about states of matter, plus read more facts and play games to practice what you know.

Every effort has been made to ensure that these websites are appropriate for children. However, because of the nature of the Internet, it is impossible to guarantee that these sites will remain active indefinitely or that their contents will not be altered.